Five Chosen Women of the Old Testament

A PRACTICAL STUDY

Deborah HS Chai

WESTBOW·
PRESS
A DIVISION OF THOMAS NELSON
& ZONDERVAN

WestBow Press books may be ordered through booksellers or by contacting:

WestBow Press
A Division of Thomas Nelson & Zondervan
1663 Liberty Drive
Bloomington, IN 47403
www.westbowpress.com
1 (866) 928-1240

ISBN: 978-1-4908-2513-7 (sc)
ISBN: 978-1-4908-2514-4 (e)

Library of Congress Control Number: 2014902042

Printed in the United States of America.

WestBow Press rev. date: 02/26/2014

1 Peter 3:4

…rather let it be the hidden person of the heart, with the incorruptible beauty of a gentle and quiet spirit, which is very precious in the sight of God. (NKJV)

Introduction

Modern women are blessed to have many others who have gone before us, in history, to learn from. We find women who have led exemplary lives documented in the Bible. This is an attempt to study, and learn from five women in the Old Testament, namely Rebekah, Rachel, Deborah, Ruth and Esther. 1 Peter 3:4 has been instrumental for me during challenging moments, reminding me of what is truly valuable in the eyes of God, and all of Scripture has been and will be 'the rock on which I stand'.

Four of the women are Jewish and one is a Moabitess, whom God chose and raised up to cling on to another Jewish woman, who became a matriach, a grandmother in substance, leading to the birth of king David, and then Jesus, many generations later.

These studies will certainly not be feminist in perspective, but will be balanced with regard to the importance of men and women. However the focus here will be on the women, and what we can learn from them, their triumphs and their failures. Let's look through the eyes of the resurrected Christ as we look at these women figures, in grace and truth (see John 1:14).

While this is a series of Bible studies primarily for women, men are welcome to study with us too, and contribute their insights :)

May the grace of our Lord Jesus, the love of the Father and the fellowship of the Holy Spirit be with us all!

Deborah Chai
August 8, 2013, Hong Kong

How to use this material

There are two main parts in this material, namely a set of questions and a set of questions with answers. Group leaders need to prepare well, with prayer and careful reading of the selected Scriptures that tell the stories of each of the five women. Group members also need to read the Scriptures and attempt the questions before discussing them in the small group. I would suggest using this material in groups of 3-6 people, with people taking turns to facilitate. It would be good training ground for future leaders.

The non-negotiables

We need to accept the Scriptures as infallible, and the character of God unquestionable, i.e. He is good, and holy, all-powerful, all-knowing, full of justice and mercy. Only then, will we be able to receive and appropriate the promises in the Bible, and walk in faith and obedience. In other words, we need to lay down any form of selfish pride, to walk in relationship with the living God.

The good news of Jesus Christ

The Christian believes that Jesus Christ is the Son of the living God, who sent Him to die on the cross for the sins of the world, and raised Him from the dead, releasing His Holy Spirit to all who would call on His name (see John 3:16). Our souls are saved for eternity, as our sins have been paid for, when Jesus gave His life on the cross. Our lives are made new, redeemed, and 'the power of cancelled sin is broken' forever. These are the words of an old hymn, which rings true for all time as Satan works hard at deceiving whoever he can deceive, and hold in bondage. We need to constantly remember that sin was cancelled when

Jesus died, and the power of sin over us is broken when we believe in this good news! We are in the world but not of the world when we submit to the Lordship of Christ, and He who is in us is greater than he who is in the world (see 1 John 4:4). We are reconciled to God and become overcomers in Christ!

Invitation

Let's look into the Word of God seriously, and determine to grow in the grace and knowledge of our Lord Jesus, as we apply God's truth in our daily lives.

Contents

1. Rebekah

Part I Marriage

We would be familiar with the life of Rebekah, her marriage story; her motherhood, found in Genesis 24, 25, 27, 28. What can we learn from her life?

1. Who is Rebekah and what can we observe about her spirit, and character from her watering the camels of a stranger? See Genesis 24: 15-25

2. What was her response/reaction when Abraham's servant revealed his intentions, by putting customary jewelery on her? See Genesis 24: 22, 28, 47

3. What kind of family did Rebekah belong to? See Genesis 24: 28-31

4. What are similarities and differences between the customs then and now? See Genesis 24: 1-14

5. What was an important qualifying attribute for the patriarch Abraham in looking for a wife for his son? Were there other specified criteria? See v. 40-44

6. How did the family send Rebekah off? See v. 59-61

7. How can we discern God's will & choice from our own inclinations, fleshly(unholy) desires? Has Abraham's servant done well?

8. What happened here? See v. 62-64

9. Was it a good and blessed union in marriage between Isaac and Rebekah? See v. 67

10. What are your views on modern courtship/relationship patterns? Finding a spouse through Christian internet dating services? Going out to meet a potential spouse, referral of family/friends?

11. What would be sound biblical guidelines?

Part II Motherhood

See Genesis 25:19-28

Isaac was 40 when he married Rebekah, and Rebekah should be around that age too, given that she is of a younger generation, and Isaac was born when Abraham was 100 years of age (Genesis 21: 5). She had been barren for twenty years, till Isaac prayed.

1. What was the pregnancy like, and what was Rebekah's course of action? See Genesis 25: 22

2. What was the message that the Lord gave? See v. 23

3. How would you respond if you were in her shoes?

4. Twins were born, just as the Lord said; how were they named? See v. 25-26

5. What was parenthood like for Isaac & Rebekah? Were they the perfect parents of the day? See v. 27-28

Like father like son, is a common saying; perhaps that was the bonding which happened naturally between Isaac and the older son Esau, a man of the outdoors, who loved to hunt, and brought back wild game for the family. However, there was strife in the home as Jacob the younger son bought the birthright of Esau with a bowl of stew (Genesis 25: 29-34). The family experienced a time of famine, and Isaac sought help from Abimelech king of Gerar, but lied to protect himself, on account of his wife's beautiful appearance. And the Lord intervened and protected his marriage (Genesis 26: 6-11)! And more strife came in when Esau married Hittite women (Genesis 26: 34).

See Genesis 27: 5-29

God knew the hearts of men and women even from the day of conception, and sure enough events unfolded according to the word that was given to Rebekah in Genesis 25:23.

6. Why did Rebekah favour Jacob and not Esau? We can think of possible reasons. See Genesis 27: 5-10, 25: 27-28

7. Can her conspiracy with her younger son be justified in anyway, as she appears to be helping God in fulfilling His word? Elaborate. What are the implications on the family/marriage relationship?

8. Would you do the same if you were in her shoes?

9. Why was the blessing so important and sought after? See Genesis 27: 28-29

10. It seems to be very difficult to identify the first point of failure, in the whole saga, and would you agree that God had chosen Jacob,

from the womb, to mold him, teach him and use him for greater purposes? Could Rebekah have known this from the beginning?

11. Are you appalled at the politicking within the family? How would the Lord Jesus speak in situations like this?

See Genesis 27: 42-46

12. When Rebekah got wind of Esau's intention to kill Jacob, what did she do? See v. 45. Was there a hint of repentance?

13. Finally we read of conversation between Rebekah and Isaac, what are the implications here? See v. 46

14. How would people respond to brokenness? What is your experience? Has good come out of the brokenness in the family of Isaac and Rebekah?

See Genesis 28: 1-5

15. What is the true tone of the blessing that Isaac pronounces on Jacob this time? See v. 3-4

16. What can we see of God's hand, His righteousness and His grace?

Read aloud:

Psalm 51: 17
The sacrifices of God are a broken spirit, a broken and a contrite heart- these O God, You will not despise. (NKJV)

Romans 8: 28-29
And we know that all things work together for good to those who love God, to those who are the called according to His purpose. For whom He foreknew, He also predestined to be conformed to the image of His Son, that He might be the firstborn among many brethren. (NKJV)

2. Rachel

Part I Marriage

See Genesis 28: 1-5 (prelude), and Genesis 29: 5-30

1. Who was Rachel? See Genesis 29: 5-6

2. What happened between Jacob and Rachel? See v. 9-12, 18

3. Jacob served Laban for seven years for Rachel, and was given Leah the older sister for his wife, due to the custom of the day. Could Rachel have done something about it? See v. 21-30

4. Jacob had to complete the week with Leah, and then was given Rachel, the one he loved, for his wife, and had to serve another seven years. How did he respond? How would you have responded if you were in his shoes/thrown into a similar situation?

5. Why do you think God allowed Jacob to be deceived?

6. What about Rachel? Could she have known that her father would resort to deception in the name of customary practice?

7. We live in the age of the new testament (new covenant); is there hope for those who married against their own will and those who suffer from pressure be it from peers or family members-- being unmarried?

Part II Motherhood

See Genesis 29: 31-35, 30: 1-25

1. We see the hand of the Lord intervene for Leah, as she was unloved. How did the Lord come through for Leah, and what does this say of His character? See Genesis 29: 31-35

2. What can we see of Leah's prayer life?

3. What was Rachel's reaction, and the implication on her character/personality? See Genesis 30: 1

4. Rachel gave her maid Bilhah to Jacob as a concubine, and she conceived twice. What happened next? See Genesis 30: 9-13

5. Can you imagine the atmosphere in the household, as the family grew?

6. Rachel asked Leah for her son's mandrakes, and paid for it by releasing Jacob. What can we see of the values practised here? See v. 14-16

7. Leah bore 3 more children and thought that she had won her husband's heart. Had she really? Comment on her constant longing to be loved, and a general phenomena among unloved women who are married. See Genesis 3: 16

8. Would you agree that Jesus the Passover Lamb, in His death and resurrection has removed/reversed the curse on man, and woman? See Romans 3: 24-26

9. The Lord heard Rachel too, and opened her womb finally, and she gave birth to Joseph (meaning: the Lord shall add to me another son). Why do you think Rachel had to wait so long to conceive? See Genesis 30: 22

10. What can we see of God's wisdom & knowledge? Do you think He is fair?

See Genesis 31: 4-16

Jacob proposes to his wives to leave Laban, after hearing from God. And they agree to leave, to return to his father's house in Canaan.

11. What is the atmosphere in the home now, at this turning point in their lives?

12. How is Laban described by his daughters Leah & Rachel? See v. 14

13. Why do you think Rachel stole the household idols before they sneaked away? See Genesis 31: 19-21

14. What are the implications and the impact of Jacob's words in v. 32-34, as he did not know that Rachel had taken her father's idols and hidden them?

15. Why do you think Rachel and her boy Joseph was positioned last when Jacob was going to face his twin brother Esau? See Genesis 33: 2-3

Genesis 34 details the daughter of Jacob, Dinah taken to bed by force by Shechem, the son of the ruler of the place, and the sons of Jacob, Simeon and Levi took revenge with deceit, killing every male, including Shechem and Hamor the prince of the land. Jacob who had remained quiet finally opened his mouth, then took action, having heard from God. See Genesis 35: 1-4. Jacob instructed his household to come clean by putting away all foreign gods which they had kept. And God spoke again to him at Bethel, affirming the promise to Abraham and Isaac, to multiply him, and to bless him. Jacob was again given the name Israel (affirmation) (see also Genesis 32: 28)

See Genesis 34: 16-20

16. Rachel suffered severe labour pains as she was giving birth, and named her son Ben-Oni (meaning the son of my sorrow), just before she died. Jacob renamed him Benjamin (the son of my right hand). What can we see here of Jacob's character?

17. Where was Rachel buried? Is there spiritual significance here?

18. If you were to summarise the life of Rachel in two words, which words would they be? Has God been present in her life? Had she known real happiness?

Part III Prophetic significance

See Jeremiah 31: 1-34

The prophet Jeremiah wrote as he was carried by the Spirit of the Living God, it was a dream/vision, where he woke up from, which he documented. See v. 26

1. In verses 1-14, what was the 'mood' of the children of Israel? What were their circumstances? Who is really in control?

2. See v. 7; how would you interpret 'remnant' in this context? Is this applicable today?

3. In v. 15, what is Rachel symbolic if here?

4. Why was she weeping?

5. What is the word of the Lord?

6. How can this apply in our daily lives today, in the church?

7. See v. 9 & 18; what is Ephraim symbolic of here?

8. What is God's heart towards Israel?

9. How does this apply in the body of believers today, we who are His sons and daughters, through Christ?

10. See v. 4, 21-22; what is the virgin of Israel symbolic of here? What could it mean that 'a woman shall compass a man' (KJV)?

11. See v. 23-25; what is God's heart in 'bringing again their captivity'?

12. See v. 28; why is it necessary that God should watch over the people to 'pluck up, break down, throw down, destroy, afflict; and then to build and to plant'?

13. See v. 29-34; what is old and what is new that the Lord is doing here?

14. What is this new covenant? See also Hebrews 7: 22-28, 8: 9-13

15. What do you need to do today, to renew your mind, and to refresh your spirit, in order to move forward in your walk with the Lord?

Our walk with God is a journey, with ups and downs, with different seasons in life that we must learn to deal with; by trusting Him, in prayer and supplication, in faith and obedience. In the lives of Rebekah and Rachel we have seen much trouble and saga in their family life, yet God was gracious, and brought them through the tough times, blessing them with increase, and protection from their enemies. Let's learn from history, and trust His Holy Spirit to guide us in the different seasons of life.

Read aloud:

Ephesians 2: 1-7
And you He made alive, who were dead in trespasses and sins, in which you once walked according to the course of this world, according to the prince of the power of the air, the spirit who now works in the sons of disobedience, among whom also we all once conducted ourselves in the lusts of our flesh, fulfilling the desires of the flesh and of the mind, and were by nature children of wrath, just as the others.

But God, who is rich in mercy, because of His great love with which He loved us, even when we were dead in trespasses, made us alive together with Christ (by grace you have been saved), and raised us up together, and made us sit together in the heavenly places in Christ Jesus, that in the ages to come He might show the exceeding riches of His grace in His kindness toward us in Christ Jesus. (NKJV)

3. Deborah

Part I The prophetic word and the battlefield

Judges 4

It was a time of rebuilding lives for the Israelites as Joshua had led them into the promised land, and last battles were fought where the tribes of Israel subdued other people groups, not driving them out completely, making them subject to forced labour instead. After the death of Joshua and his generation, the new generation that grew up did not know God and did evil, and served the Baals, following the culture of the people of the land. God allowed stronger enemies to overpower His people, and raised judges to bring deliverance (see Judges 2: 10-16).

Deborah was a judge who held court in the hill country of Ephraim, she was also a prophetess, and a wife, married to Lappidoth (see Judges 4: 4-5).

1. What was the condition of the people of Israel? See Judges 4: 1-3

2. What transpired between Deborah and Barak in Judges 4: 6-8?

3. What was Barak's reaction and what was the consequence? See v. 9 & 10

4. What's a good lesson here for men to take home?

5. What is the role of prophecy/the prophetess and the general? See v. 14-16

6. The leader of the enemy's camp, Sisera fled on foot after his troops were defeated. Where did he end up? See v. 17

7. Who were Jael and Heber? See v. 11, 17

8. How did Jael deal with Sisera? See v. 18-21

9. What do you think led Jael to be on the side of God's people, Barak and the Israelite troops? See v. 22

10. What was the ultimate end of Jabin? See v. 23 & 24

11. What does Jabin represent? See v. 2-3. What is the moral of the story here?

12. Do you observe similarities between the time of the judges, and the time we are living in now?

13. What could be a personal lesson/application for you?

Part II The song

Judges 5

1. What event brings about praise to the Lord? See v. 2

2. What was the context, before Deborah arose as a mother in Israel? What was the problem? See v. 7 & 8

3. How was the condition of the heart, of Deborah? See v. 9

4. What was the role of the singers? See v. 10-12

5. How did the tribes of Israel respond to the call to battle? See v. 13-18

6. What is being described in v. 19-30?

7. Whose victory was it really? See v. 31

8. What is your view/understanding of the prophetic gifting?

9. What are underlying principles that should accompany the gift of prophecy? See 1 Corinthians 14: 3, 19-20. See also 1 John 4: 1-3

10. How can the church today carry out the exercise of prophecy as instructed by the apostle Paul in 1 Corinthians 14: 29-31. What is a key principle here?

The gift of prophecy makes us stronger, and prepares us for tough times. Conflict and oppression is real in both the physical and spiritual realm, and is often inter-related. But God has cared for His people, and has proven His love and faithfulness in the Old Testament and in the New Testament. Today we have the Word of God, a treasure trove for all who would take it seriously, and apply it. It is good to ask ourselves every now and then: Am I growing in the fruit of the Spirit and in the gifts of the Spirit?

Read aloud:

Revelation 12: 10-12
Then I heard a loud voice saying in heaven, "Now salvation, and strength, and the kingdom of our God, and the power of His Christ has come, for the accuser of our brethren, who accused them before our God day and night, has been cast down. And they overcame him by the blood of the Lamb and by the word of their testimony, and they did not love their lives to the death. Therefore rejoice O heavens, and you who dwell in them! Woe to the inhabitants of the earth and the sea! For the devil has come down to you, having great wrath, because he knows that he has a short time." (NKJV)

Revelation 21: 7
He who overcomes shall inherit all things, and I will be his God and he shall be my son. (NKJV)

4. Ruth

Part I From despondency to hope

Ruth 1 & 2

This piece of history is set in the period of the judges, where there was famine in Judah, and an Ephrathite from Bethlehem, Elimelech, and his family went to live in Moab. Elimelech died, leaving his wife Naomi and his sons, Mahlon and Kilion who married Moabite women. They had lived in Moab for about ten years, and Naomi's two sons died too. She heard of better prospects in Bethlehem, as the Lord provided food for His people there, and decided to go back (Ruth 1: 6).

1. At the crossroads, what was Naomi's counsel & prayer for her daughters-in-law? See Ruth 1: 8-9

2. What was their reaction? See v. 9-10

3. What was the culture of the day when one's husband has died? And what seems to be the role of the woman in general? See v. 11-13

4. What was the outcome at the crossroads finally? See v. 14-18

5. What is evident from Ruth's response to her mother-in-law? See v. 16-17

6. What was the meaning of the name 'Naomi'? What was the condition of her heart upon arriving in her hometown, as she was greeted by her old friends? See v. 20-21

7. What season was it when Naomi and Ruth returned to Bethlehem? See v. 22

8. What can you see from Ruth's actions? See Ruth 2: 1-3

9. What is evident from the exchange between Boaz and his harvesters? See v. 4-7

10. Boaz went to speak with Ruth, and showed her kindness. See v. 8-13; how was Ruth's response?

11. What can we learn here about position/ethnic background and its implications, comparing what we see in general in today's society, with the way Boaz had treated Ruth? See v. 14-16

12. What did Ruth bring back to her mother-in-law? See v. 17-18

13. What was Naomi's reaction upon finding out that Ruth went to work in the fields that belonged to Boaz? See v. 20-22

Part II Marriage and genealogy

Ruth 3 & 4

1. What was the intention behind Naomi's instructions to Ruth? See Ruth 3: 1-4

2. What was Ruth's response? See v. 5-6

3. What was a key statement in the words of Ruth to Boaz? See v. 8-9

4. What was Boaz's response? See v. 10-13

5. What was the significance of the gift of barley for Ruth to take home? See v. 15

6. What can we observe from Naomi's advice? See v. 18

7. Boaz went to the town gate and got ten elders together, and invited the other kinsman-redeemer to settle the estate of Elimelech. What can we see from his attitude and his actions? See Ruth 4: 1-5

8. What was the outcome? See v. 6-10

9. What was the blessing from the elders and all those present? See v. 11

10. Boaz married Ruth and she conceived, and gave birth to a son. How did the women praise God? See v. 15

11. In the genealogy, Boaz was the ancestor of king David. His grandmother was Rahab (the ex-prostitute), and his wife a Moabite who chose to worship Yahweh. What can we see here of God's heart, toward the naming of 'His people'? See Matthew 1: 1-6, Genesis 12: 1-3

The major theme that runs through the book of Ruth is God's grace and kindness. Kindness begets kindness (evident from the relationship between Naomi and Ruth, then Ruth and Boaz). God is ever so ready to bless those who seek His face, those who would return to Him and walk in faith and obedience. He is Jehovah-Jireh, caring and providing for those who would trust Him. God provided for Ruth and Naomi a kinsman-redeemer and provided for Boaz, a wife. And today we can trust the Lord Jesus, our redeemer and coming King, as we walk with Him and partner with Him, committing the work of our hands to Him.

Read aloud:

Psalm 90: 15-17
Make us glad according to the days in which you have afflicted us, the years in which we have seen evil. Let Your work appear to Your servants, and Your glory to their children. And let the beauty of the Lord our God be upon us, and establish the work of our hands for us; yes, establish the work of our hands. (NKJV)

5. Esther

Part I The fall of a queen and the making of another

Esther 1 & 2

1. What was the context described in Esther 1: 1-8?

2. What was Queen Vashti engaged in and how did she respond to the king's wishes? See v. 9-12

3. What were the consequences, and what do you think was the likely reason that led to the consequences? See v. 13-20

4. What is a good lesson here for women, especially those who are married?

5. What was the edict that was proclaimed after the removal of the queen? See v. 22

6. How was the king feeling and what advice did he receive from his attendants? See Esther 2: 1-4

7. Who was Mordecai and Esther (Hadassah)? See v. 5-7

8. What happened to Esther, what was her attitude, and the resulting outcome? See v. 8-9

9. How was her relationship with Mordecai? See v. 10-11

10. What were the customs in the palace for women who were chosen to vie for the position of the queen? See v. 12-14

11. How was the relationship between Esther and Hegai, and the other attendants in the palace?

12. How did the king take to Esther? See v. 16-17

13. How was the coronation celebrated? See v. 18

14. Why was it imperative for Esther's nationality to be kept secret? See v. 20

15. What did Mordecai uncover when sitting at the king's gate, and what did he do? See v. 21-22

16. What was the outcome? See v. 23

Part II The plight of the Jews

Esther 3, 4 & 5

1. For some reason, Haman the Agagite was honoured by the king, and people were commanded to kneel down and pay honour to him, as the king had made him second in rank, higher than all the other nobles in the land. Why do you think Mordecai refused to follow the instructions? See Esther 3: 1-4

2. How did Haman react? See v. 5-6

3. What did Haman propose to the king, and on what pretext was it proposed? See v. 8-9

4. How did the king respond? See v. 10-11

5. What was the edict proclaimed over the Jews? See v. 12-13

6. As the king and Haman sat down to drink, what happened in the city of Susa? See v. 15

7. How did Mordecai and his people react? See Esther 4: 1-3

8. How did Esther react when she heard that Mordecai was wailing in sackcloth? See v. 4-5

9. What was Mordecai's urgent request to Esther? See v. 8

10. Esther sent word of her situation to Mordecai, which had seemed hopeless as she had not been in the king's presence for 30 days; what was Mordecai's challenge to her? See v. 13-14

11. Did Esther take up the challenge? See v. 15-17

12. What was the implication here, as Esther instructed Mordecai and all the Jews in Susa to fast with her and her maids for three days?

13. What did Esther do on the third day? See Esther 5: 1

14. What was the king's response? See v. 2-3

15. Esther did not bat an eyelid at the offer of power over half of Xerxes' kingdom. What can you observe here of her character? See v. 4

16. Esther invited the king to bring Haman to an banquet, and promised to make her request known. How was Haman's attitude? See v. 11-12

17. What was gnawing at his mind, what advice did his wife and his friends give him? See v. 13-14

Part III The honour of a hero and the hanging of a villain

Esther 6 & 7

1. King Xerxes could not sleep and read the book of the chronicles. What was he reminded of? See Esther 6: 1-3

2. What did the king proceed to do? See v. 4-10

3. Who do you think was behind the whole orchestration of events here? See v. 11-14

4. At Esther's banquet, the king again offered to do for Esther whatever she asked; what did she ask for? See Esther 7: 1-4

5. How did the king respond? See v. 5-7

6. What did he see when returning from the palace garden? See v. 8

7. Harbona, one of the attending eunuchs voluntarily announced a possible punishment for Haman; does it surprise you as he seems to have been waiting for the chance to tell of what Haman had done? See v. 9-10

8. What had been a weakness of the king which made him vulnerable to the manipulation of those with evil intent?

Part IV Deliverance and celebration

Esther 8, 9 & 10

1. What did Esther continue to do, and how was her heart towards her people? See Esther 8: 1-6

2. What was the king's instructions? See v. 8-10

3. What was granted to the Jews in the new edict, on the same day on which they had been sold for destruction?

4. How did Mordecai leave the palace having accomplished his duties, and how did the people in the city respond to the new edict? See v. 15-16

5. How had the tables turned for the Jews when the thirteenth day of the month of Adar came? What was Mordecai's role? See Esther 9: 1-4

6. Why do you think the Jews chose not to take the plunder? See v. 10, 15-16

7. The king again offered to do whatever Esther requested; what was her request? See v. 13-15

8. What is the significance of Purim, and how was it celebrated? See v. 18-22

9. What was the final end for Xerxes and Mordecai? See Esther 10: 1-3

Time and truth reveals much about justice and mercy, as Esther had been queen for 4 years, and while evildoers scheme destruction for the Jews, God's plan of deliverance was being worked out simultaneously, as his people worshiped Him and obeyed Him. Haman received justice that was due to him, and Xerxes received God's mercy, releasing mercy to the Jews, by revoking his decree to destroy them.

One Bible scholar and teacher, Pawson, points out that the whole turn of events showed how faithful our God is, as the deliverance of the Jews, made it possible for the Messiah to be born hundreds of years later, in Bethlehem.

Read aloud, the following Scripture which is prophetic and describes the coming of our Lord Jesus:

Psalm 45: 4-7
In your majesty, ride forth victoriously on behalf of truth, humility and righteousness; let your right hand display awesome deeds. Let your sharp arrows pierce the hearts of the king's enemies; let the nations fall beneath your feet. Your throne O God, will last forever and ever; a sceptre of justice will be the sceptre of your kingdom. You love righteousness and hate wickedness; therefore God your God, has set you above your companions by anointing you with the oil of joy. (NIV)

6. Rebekah

Part I Marriage

We would be familiar with the life of Rebekah, her marriage story; her motherhood, found in Genesis 24, 25, 27. What can we learn from her life?

1. Who is Rebekah and what can we observe about her spirit, and character from her watering the camels of a stranger? See Genesis 24:15-25.

    Daughter of Bethuel, son of Nahor, Abraham's brother. Rebekah was kind, hardworking and considerate as she watered the camels, and also drew water for the men.

2. What was her response/reaction when Abraham's servant revealed his intentions, by putting customary jewelery on her? See Genesis 24:22, 28, 47

    She ran home and announced it to her household! And brought Abraham's servant home with her. She was generous in spirit in offering straw & fodder for the camels and shelter for the men. There must have been some recognition in the spirit, of something familiar & common – e.g. faith in the Almighty God evident in the conversation.

3. What kind of family did Rebekah belong to? See Genesis 24:28-31

    Close-knit, wealthy, God-fearing, Jewish…the brother Laban seeing the nose-ring & bracelets on Rebekah must have understood the marriage proposal.

4. What are similarities and differences between the customs then and now? See Genesis 24:1-14

The Chinese customs are similar…where there is gift of jewelery(& lots of other goodies!) as a mark of choice, and covenant in the betrothal. Difference…no diamond rings then! Societal values, and systems have evolved a fair bit…families were a lot stronger then. Yet Rebekah was given the final choice to marry or not to marry. In today's democratic free markets, the idea of contract instead of covenant may have become too strong; where people view marriage like business. Like=stay married. Dislike=divorce. What a sad phenomena that keeps some lawyers thriving in business!

5. What was an important qualifying attribute for the patriarch Abraham in looking for a wife for his son? Were there other specified criteria? See v. 40-44

She must not be a Canaanite, and must be a relative; implying that she must be God-fearing…as the Jews then kept to their creed, their faith in the Almighty God.

6. How did the family send Rebekah off? See v. 59-61

With a nurse, attendants and a 'prayer blessing' bidding her to increase, blessing her offspring as well. Interestingly, Rebekah and her attendants mounted the camels which she had watered. She had no inkling that the camels were prepared for her, and her attendants.

7. How can we discern God's will & choice from our own inclinations, fleshly(unholy) desires? Has Abraham's servant done well?

Yes he has. He submitted to God his assignment, and asked God for signs which materialised. He had the wisdom and insight to look for kindness, diligence and generosity. Confirmation was final when the family agreed, and Rebekah herself agreed. The Spirit always bears witness in our spirit by releasing peace, when a decision is made, when it is in His will.

8. What happened here? See v.62-64

Rebekah confirmed the identity of Isaac, and covered herself. Isaac would have known that Rebekah was his bride-to-be when he sighted the family servant, and the company of men, and women on camels.

9. Was it a good and blessed union in marriage between Isaac and Rebekah? See v. 67

Yes, it was uncomplicated, as Rebekah was loved and after the death of Sarah, Isaac's mother, she was a source of comfort and companionship for her husband.

10. What are your views on modern courtship/relationship patterns? Finding a spouse through Christian internet dating services? Going out to meet a potential spouse, referral of family/friends?

Some could raise very liberal points on courtship, e.g. co-habitation to test the waters. And views will differ on going out with different people to get to know each one better. This tends to be quite personal. The biblical principle of utmost importance here would be faithfulness to God and one's witness through conduct and conversation. The key question to ask oneself is: will my actions compromise these principles, and bring grief and pain o the heart of God, others and self?

11. What would be sound biblical guidelines?

The choice of a spouse should not be too hard…when a man or woman is totally surrendered in his/her walk with God, worshipping Him in spirit and in truth (John 4:24), and marriage is a gift in that person's life (James 1:17). There should be mutual agreement on direction, growing together, serving God and reaching out to others. E.g. direction would mean the choice to pray and listen to the Holy Spirit, to walk closer with God everyday, not further away from Him. Simply because God would lead us to profit, and not to destruction (see Isaiah 48:17)

Part II Motherhood

See Genesis 25:19-28

Isaac was 40 when he married Rebekah, and Rebekah should be around that age too, given that she is of a younger generation, and Isaac was born when Abraham was 100 years of age. (Genesis 21:5) She had been barren for twenty years, till Isaac prayed.

1. What was the pregnancy like, and what was Rebekah's course of action? See Genesis 25: 22

   She inquired of the Lord. In other words she prayed and asked the Lord.

2. What was the message that the Lord gave? See v. 23

   It was a prophetic word...making her a mother of two nations. Probably quite staggering.

3. How would you respond if you were in her shoes?

   Turn speechless for a few days?! I would certainly be praying and listening.

4. Twins were born, just as the Lord said, how were they named? See v. 25-26

   They were named according to their physical appearance (Esau-hairy), behavioural traits (Jacob-supplanter).

5. What was parenthood like for Isaac & Rebekah? Were they the perfect parents of the day? See v. 27-28

   It must have been a challenge, and they each had a favourite son. They were not perfect parents, and today many would have made the same mistakes.

Like father like son, is a common saying; perhaps that was the bonding which happened naturally between Isaac and the older son Esau, a man of the outdoors, who loved to hunt, and brought back wild game for the family. However, there was strife in the home as Jacob the younger son bought the birthright of Esau with a bowl of stew (Genesis 25: 29-34). The family experienced a time of famine, and Isaac sought help from Abimelech king of Gerar, but lied to protect himself, on account of his wife's beautiful appearance. And the Lord intervened and protected his marriage(Genesis 26: 6-11)! And more strife came in when Esau married Hittite women (Genesis 26: 34).

See Genesis 27:5-29

God knew the hearts of men and women even from the day of conception, and sure enough events unfolded as the word that was given to Rebekah in Genesis 25:23.

6. Why did Rebekah favour Jacob and not Esau? We can think of possible reasons. See v. 27.

   Perhaps simply because of the time he spent at home with her. Jacob was plain (KJV), mild (NKJV), peaceful (NASB), quiet (The Message).

7. Can her conspiracy with her younger son be justified in anyway, as she appears to be helping God in fulfilling His word? Elaborate. What are the implications on the family/marriage relationship?

   No, it could not be justified, as God who had prepared to bless the younger son must have His perfect way, time or place to do so.

This conspiracy resulted in the family break-up, with Esau running off, and Isaac probably heart-broken. The strained family/marriage relationship went from bad to worse.

8. Would you do the same if you were in her shoes?

Let each one go home and pray, think and settle this with the Almighty in her own quiet time!

9. Why was the blessing so important and sought after? See v. 28-29

Patriarch blessings are customary, and words have great power in them, especially that of a spiritual leader, parent. For Rebekah, it appears that her love for Jacob drove her to conspire with him to get hold of the blessing. She could have spoken directly with Isaac about the word that God gave her earlier. Then reverence for God and respect for her husband would have been present.

10. It seems to be very difficult to identify the first point of failure, in the whole saga, and would you agree that God had chosen Jacob, from the womb, to mould him, teach him and use him for greater purposes? Could Rebekah have known this from the beginning?

God had chosen Jacob from the womb as in Genesis 25:23, yet Rebekah had forgotten, and took things into her own hands, even willing to be cursed; showing how desperate and despondent she had become, as she had lost focus on God and His righteousness. The challenge for women is to focus on God, and His ways, to choose to become more like Jesus everyday, humble, gentle, reverent and respectful.

11. Are you appalled at the politicking within the family? How would the Lord Jesus speak in situations like this?

Interestingly, the point of contention is the patriarch blessing, which brings with it the power /responsibility to guard the family and everything that they have. Modern day wealthy families face similar challenges in modern times. Jesus would say: ...Man shall not live by bread alone, but by every word that proceeds from the mouth of God (Matthew 4:4). And to counter fear, Jesus gives peace, with truth: ...Peace I leave with you, My peace I give to you; not as the world gives do I give to you. Let not your heart be troubled, neither let it be afraid (John 14:27).

See Genesis 27:42-46

12. When Rebekah got wind of Esau's intention to kill Jacob, what did she do? See v. 45. Was there a hint of repentance?

She instructed Jacob to go and find refuge in her brother Laban's house. In v. 45 she realises her love for Esau her other son, and expresses her desire to keep them both by her side, no more favouritism, finally. Yes, she had repented.

13. Finally we read of conversation between Rebekah and Isaac, what are the implications here? See v. 46.

Rebekah confesses her pain, that came from the foreign women whom Esau had taken as wives, and places trust in her husband. The marriage was mending, being healed.

14. How would people respond to brokenness? What is your experience? Has good come out out of the brokenness in the family of Isaac and Rebekah?

Some could spiral downward into emotional deadlock(blame, shame, hatred, bitterness, self-pity) but those who come to God for deliverance, with humble and contrite hearts receive deliverance, mercy and truth. Yes the Almighty must have intervened and brought a change of heart, and good has come out of the brokenness and painful experience.

See Genesis 28:1-5

15. What is the true tone of the blessing that Isaac pronounces on Jacob this time? See v. 3-4.

    It is one of peace and confidence, without the shadow of a doubt/ intrigue.

16. What can we see of God's hand, His righteousness and His grace?

    It's there even when we feel horrible, forsaken, despondent, hopeless. His Presence brings healing and deliverance.

7. Rachel

Part 1 Marriage

See Genesis 28:1-5 (prelude), and Genesis 29:5-30

1. Who was Rachel? See Genesis 29: 5-6

    Rachel was the daughter of Laban, and she was a shepherdess. Laban was the brother of Rebekah, Jacob's mother.

2. What happened between Jacob and Rachel? See v. 9-12, 18

    Jacob saw Rachel coming with the sheep to the well, and rolled away the stone, and watered the sheep. He kissed her, and then wept, and revealed his identity. She ran home and told her dad. He fell in love with Rachel and agreed to work for Laban seven years for her hand in marriage.

3. Jacob served Laban for seven years for Rachel, and was given Leah the older sister for his wife, due to the custom of the day. Could Rachel have done something about it? See v. 21-30

    Customarily speaking, no. But people might speculate and come up with all sorts of answers, e.g. they could have eloped. This can be an opportunity for a light moment.

4. Jacob had to complete the week with Leah, and then was given Rachel, the one he loved, for his wife, and had to serve another seven

years. How did he respond? How would you have responded if you were in his shoes/thrown into a similar situation?

He submitted to the wishes of Laban, and worked another seven years. He was determined and knew what he really wanted. He knew the Lord, and therefore there must have been a measure of grace that came from God.

5. Why do you think God allowed Jacob to be deceived?

It must have been part of his life training, to become a patriach, there would be more heartbreak to come later, especially when his sons deceived him, after selling Joseph to an Egyptian. Some will probably say that God allowed him to have a taste of his own medicine! Surely it was a maturing process.

6. What about Rachel? Could she have known that her father would resort to deception in the name of customary practice?

She could have known her father's ways, but there was little that she could have done, as 'parents had the last word'. In today's context, many would have fallen into self-pity, and rebelled.

7. We live in the age of the new testament (new covenant); is there hope for those who married against their own will and those who suffer from pressure be it from peers or family members-- being unmarried?

Marriage is often a channel where self has to come secondary, and many happy marriages have been borne out of self-sacrifice, more than romance. Often it involves a death to self-will, a choice to honour God, family, and covenant.

Some in life are called to singleness, and for some it is a choice. See 1 Corinthians 7:7, Matthew 19:10-12; ultimately whatever one receives as a gift from God is good!

Part II Motherhood

See Genesis 29:31-35, 30:1-25

1. We see the hand of the Lord intervene for Leah, as she was unloved. How did the Lord come through for Leah, and what does this say of His character? See Genesis 29:31-35.

   God had compassion, and intervened, as He knew her suffering. What Jacob could not give her, would be relieved through her childbearing, and her motherhood.

2. What can we see of Leah's prayer life?

   It was real, and it gave her comfort.

3. What was Rachel's reaction, and the implication on her character/personality? See Genesis 30:1

   Rachel looked to her husband, and it was immature of her, and she got reprimanded. Growing up with physical beauty would have made her beauty the envy/admiration of many, possibly given her false security, and comfort, which impeded her growth as a person.

4. Rachel gave her maid Bilhah to Jacob as a concubine, and she conceived twice. What happened next? See Genesis 30: 9-13.

   Leah followed suit, and gave her maid Zilpah to be Jacob's concubine, and she too conceived twice.

5. Can you imagine the atmosphere in the household, as the family grew?

   Yes, it was competitive, and scandalous, while the household grew.

6. Rachel asked Leah for her son's mandrakes, and paid for it by releasing Jacob. What can we see of the values being practised here? See v. 14-16

Rachel was a schemer, using worldly wisdom to get what she wanted, and did not put her husband first.

7. Leah bore 3 more children and thought that she had won her husband's heart. Had she really? Comment on her constant longing to be loved, and a general phenomena among unloved women who are married. See Genesis 3:16.

It was a most natural thing for Leah to yearn after her husband, as she was married to him, and this was a spiritual law (unfortunately a curse after the fall) according to Genesis 3:16.

8. Would you agree that Jesus the Passover Lamb, in His death and resurrection has removed/reversed the curse on man and woman? See Romans 3:24-26.

Certainly! Thank God for sending Jesus to reverse the curse on man and woman, our lives are redeemed, and we live under His grace and power, and He has made us overcomers. When work is difficult, He empowers us to overcome, when relationships are difficult, He empowers us to overcome by His Holy Spirit. God is active among us today, and many have experienced minimal pain in natural childbearing- this is a sure sign of His grace, and redemptive Presence. And marriage which is Christ-centred where the man and woman both look first to God for wholeness, grace and truth has better chances of happiness, the woman especially need not look to her husband for fulfillment, but looks to support and help him as per original design, drawing her strength from the Lord. And a husband in his right mind would be thankful, and affirm such a wife, and give glory to God.

9. The Lord heard Rachel too, and opened her womb finally, and she gave birth to Joseph (meaning: The Lord shall add to me another son). Why do you think Rachel had to wait so long, to conceive? See Genesis 30:22.

I believe He wanted Rachel to learn patience/long-suffering. When the time was ripe she was rewarded.

10. What can we see of God's wisdom & knowledge? Do you think He is fair?

Our Father in heaven is sovereign, omniscient, fair, and loves each one with no favoritism! We can see His grace and love toward Leah, Rachel & Jacob as the family grew.

See Genesis 31:4-16

Jacob proposes to his wives to leave Laban, after hearing from God. And they agree to leave, to return to his father's house in Canaan.

11. What is the atmosphere in the home now, at this turning point in their lives?

There was a lot more grace and peace, as there was agreement, in preparing for their journey back to where Jacob had come from.

12. How is Laban described by his daughters Leah & Rachel? See v. 14.

They thought little of him, as he had 'sold them and devoured their money', treating them like strangers. A heartless money-monger.

13. Why do you think Rachel stole the household idols before they sneaked away? See Genesis 31:19-21

She might have wanted revenge on her dad, to spite him for all that he had done previously.

14. What are the implications and the impact of Jacob's words in v.32-34, as he did not know that Rachel had taken her father's idols and hidden them?

    Implication: Rachel made a grave mistake stealing the idols, and did not confer with Jacob; impact: she had to bear a curse from her own husband who believed that no one in his household had taken the idols.

15. Why do you think Rachel and her boy Joseph was positioned last when Jacob was going to face his twin brother Esau? See Genesis 33:2-3

    Jacob was afraid of losing her, and his son Joseph, when he would face his brother who had every reason to be angry with him for his past trespasses. It is evidence of how important Rachel was to him.

Genesis 34 details the daughter of Jacob, Dinah taken to bed by force by Shechem, the son of the ruler of the place, and the sons of Jacob, Simeon and Levi took revenge with deceit, killing every male, including Shechem and Hamor the prince of the land. Jacob who had remained quiet finally opened his mouth, then took action, having heard from God. See Genesis 35:1-4. Jacob instructed his household to come clean by putting away all foreign gods which they had kept. And God spoke again to him at Bethel, affirming the promise to Abraham and Isaac, to multiply him, and to bless him. Jacob was again given the name Israel (affirmation)(see also Genesis 32:28).

See Genesis 34:16-20

16. Rachel suffered severe labour pains as she was giving birth, and named her son Ben-Oni (meaning the son of my sorrow), just before she died. Jacob renamed him Benjamin (the son of my right hand). What can we see here of Jacob's character?

    He did not want his son to bear the stigma of pain with the old name, he was loving and kind to his youngest son.

17. Where was Rachel buried? Is there spiritual significance here?

Rachel was buried in Bethlehem, the town where Jesus would be born of a virgin. Bethlehem was a small town, and the death of Rachel marked the end of a season for the family. Jesus' birth in this seemingly insignificant town marks it's importance, in history and in God's kingdom, making clear the grace, mercy, and righteousness of our Father God- no town is too insignificant in His eyes. More discussion on Rachel's life being under the yoke of religion/custom vs. the birth of Jesus bringing the new covenant into effect will be good here.

18. If you were to summarise the life of Rachel in two words, which words would they be? Has God been present in her life? Had she known real happiness?

Turbulent, but blessed. Yes, God had opened her womb, and had been present, in love and discipline. Yet she probably did not know true happiness till very late in life, as she had struggled constantly to have her own way. However, God in His grace uses Rachel as a symbol of a mother in Israel, in Jeremiah 31-- the mother of the twelve tribes, as the relationship between Jacob and Rachel was real, based on love and truth. She had faith and her prayer life was real, acknowledging that her son was a gift from God.

Part III Prophetic significance

Jeremiah 31:1-34

The prophet Jeremiah writes as he was carried by the Spirit of the Living God, it was a dream/vision, where he woke up from, which he documented. See v. 26.

1. In verses 1-14, what was the 'mood' of the children of Israel? What were their circumstances? Who is really in control?

   It was sad, as they had been taken into slavery by their captors, to a foreign land. But God was still in control, and loves His people with an everlasting love, see v. 3, and promises to deliver. They would cry out to Him, and hope in His deliverance.

2. See v. 7; how would you interpret 'remnant' in this context? Is this applicable today?

   God would raise a group of his chosen ones (left of the sword) to return to Israel in the fullness of time. And yes today, taking Israel to mirror the church, God is raising true believers, purifying the faith of many (Malachi 3:3), so that we would be the remnant proclaiming His love and truth without compromise, accelerating awakening and revival, where He would place us.

3. In verse 15, what is Rachel symbolic of here?

   A mother weeping for her children who had been lost/taken captive.

4. Why was she weeping?

   She was weeping in pain for her own suffering and the suffering of her children.

5. What is the word of the Lord?

   Weep no more. They will return.

6. How can this apply in our daily lives today, in the church?

   Intercessors/spiritual moms/mentors who keep watch day and night, sometimes with weeping, can be encouraged, as the Lord hears the prayers of the righteous (James 5: 16). Bondages of addiction, disease, immaturity can be broken, and lives can be restored in fullness. Sometimes, it takes much patience and wisdom to pray and wait actively-keep obeying Him in present little things.

7. See verses 9 & 18; what is Ephraim symbolic of here?

The favoured and chosen of Israel, blessed of God and man, having been enslaved, disciplined, praying for strength to turn away from wickedness, believing in His grace and strength. The remnant children of Israel, who would fear(revere) the Lord, and walk with Him in faith and obedience.

8. What is God's heart towards Israel?

God's heart is as a father who longs for his children.

9. How does this apply in the body of believers today, we who are His sons and daughters, through Christ?

God's heart is as a father to us, and through Christ has torn the veil of religion, ritual and custom, loves to hear us and relate to us through His Word and His Spirit.

10. See v. 4, 21-22; what is the virgin of Israel symbolic of here? What could it mean that 'a woman shall compass a man'(KJV)?

In other prophetic writings, e.g. Hosea & Isaiah, and earlier chapters of Jeremiah (see chapter 3), Israel has been pictured as a whore, who was not faithful to her husband(Yahweh), who loved her as a wife; yet in this passage, she is seen as a 'virgin' especially in v. 4, where the Lord promises to build/strengthen her. In v. 21-22, she is exhorted to turn again to her cities, to return home, and cease from backsliding. God is doing a new thing- breaking traditions, bringing back equality between men and women, and establishing the new covenant. One prayer warrior has interpreted 'a woman shall compass a man' as the woman protecting her husband with her prayers. This could also apply to the ministry of intercession (which somehow seems to be a calling for many women), protecting the work of the men/church leadership/marketplace leadership (where the majority are men).

11. See v. 23-25; what is God's heart in 'bringing again their captivity'?

God's heart is to bring them out of slavery, and to restore joy, blessing and holiness in their midst. There will be times of peace, and their souls will be made fat-- no separation between the spiritual and secular, His people would truly know His Presence and His blessings/provisions.

12. See v. 28; why is it necessary that God should watch over the people to 'pluck up, break down, throw down, destroy, afflict; and then to build and to plant?

There were things which were not good, e.g. idols, evil practices which displeased Him, which had to be dealt with. And thereafter the Lord would build and plant on good soil, strong and clean foundations.

13. See v. 29-34; what is old and what is new that the Lord is doing here?

The old covenant had a law/curse which was carried down the generations—the offspring would suffer for the sins of his/her parent; but that is being done away with as the new covenant comes into effect.

14. What is this new covenant? See also Hebrews 7:22-28, 8:9-13.

God would forgive the sins of His people and remember them no more. He has made the way possible through Jesus, His life, death and resurrection.

15. What do you need to do today, to renew your mind, and to refresh your spirit, in order to move forward in your walk with the Lord?

A personal question for one to bring home for reflection and action, but if the atmosphere is conducive, answers can be shared in the small group.

8. Deborah

Part I The prophetic word and the battlefield

Judges 4

It was a time of rebuilding lives for the Israelites as Joshua had led them into the promised land, and last battles were fought where the tribes of Israel subdued other people groups, not driving them out completely, making them subject to forced labour instead. After the death of Joshua and his generation, the new generation that grew up did not know God and did evil, and served the Baals, following the culture of the people of the land. God allowed stronger enemies to overpower His people, and raised judges to bring deliverance (See Judges 2:10-16).

Deborah was a judge who held court in the hill country of Ephraim, and she was also a prophetess, and a wife, married to Lappidoth (See Judges 4:4-5).

1. What was the condition of the people of Israel? See Judges 4:1-3

    They did evil in God's eyes, and so God allowed twenty years of cruel oppression by Jabin, a king of Canaan, and the commander of his army Sisera, till they cried to the Lord for help.

2. What transpired between Deborah and Barak in Judges 4:6-8?

    Deborah received instruction from the Lord, that He will give the enemy into the hands of Barak, instructing him to take ten thousand men of Naphtali and Zebulun to Mount Tabor and God would lure Sisera to the Kishon River, where He would grant victory over Sisera.

3. What was Barak's reaction and what was the consequence? See v. 9 & 10

He made his obedience conditional upon Deborah going with him into battle, and the prophetess agreed and revealed the consequential outcome- where honour would no longer be his, as God would hand the enemy over to a woman.

4. What's a good lesson here for men to take home?

Trust the heart of God completely, and make every effort to know Him, and to hear from Him. Trust also the character of the prophetess, and the word of instruction for the good of the nation. (Some may answer: take time to wait on God before responding, which is surely acceptable to God Himself...there was no description of time between these exchanges.) Barak might have been hasty and sloppy out of unbelief/fear/distrust. Probably worthwhile to draw comparison between Barak and Lappidoth, while little was said of Lappidoth, he must have been a man of faith, trusting God and his wife, being partner in the pursuit of God's will. He knew his place of security.

5. What is the role of prophecy/the prophetess and the general? See v. 14-16

Prophecy in this context was directive, and specific, giving instruction to the general (Barak) to go into battle and defeat the enemy. The prophetess was God's mouthpiece. God's will was clear-- deliverance for His people.

6. The leader of the enemy's camp, Sisera fled on foot after his troops were defeated. Where did he end up? See v. 17

He fled into the tent of Jael, the wife of Heber the Kenite, thinking it was a safe place due to friendly relations between Jabin and Heber.

7. Who were Jael and Heber? See v. 11, 17

They were Kenites descended from Hobab, Moses' brother-in-law, and had friendly relations with Jabin, king of Hazor.

8. How did Jael deal with Sisera? See v. 18-21

She made him comfortable, gave him a drink, and covered him up. After he was fast asleep from exhaustion, she drove a tent peg through his temple into the ground and killed him.

9. What do you think led Jael to be on the side of God's people, Barak and the Israelite troops? See v. 22

She must have had a standard of righteousness, and knew that the ways of Jabin and Sisera were cruel and evil. There must have been something different among God's people-- the presence of God, I'd reckon.

10. What was the ultimate end of Jabin? See v. 23 & 24

His power was broken, with the death of his general, and the Israelites eventually destroyed him.

11. What does Jabin represent? See v. 2-3. What is the moral of the story here?

Jabin represents evil/satanic forces that God allows in the lives of His people for the purpose of discipline. It was for the good and repentance of His people that He allowed evil and suffering. And He can use/raise **anyone** to accomplish His will and purposes, and to receive honour.

12. Do you observe similarities between the time of the judges, and the time we are living in now?

The life of the Christian is beset with temptation and trials, as the prince of the air continues to work hard at tripping up, robbing the Christian of his/her faith. Spiritual battles that we go through are parallel to physical battles in the Old Testament, in the clash of good against evil. God's standard of righteousness has not changed-He is holy. God's people will undergo persecution (when we walk in His will), or suffering (when we sin).

13. What could be a personal lesson/application for you?

I would cry out to God at all times, I would worship Him in spirit and truth, and trust and obey Him, knowing that He is Love! God's people should remember His character, His sovereignty and walk in His ways. He has made us in His image and and has redeemed our lives with the life of His Son Jesus. Lord help us to remember that which we should remember (the ways of God) and forget that which we should forget (the ways of Egypt)! See 1 John 4:4 "You dear children, are from God and have overcome them, because the one who is in you is greater than the one who is in the world." I would feed on the Word of God, which is pure and life-giving, and place all hope and expectations in Him. The apostle John exhorts us to stay away from false teaching in his letters, and to hold on to love and truth. See also Revelation 12:10-12.

Part II The song

Judges 5

1. What event brings about praise to the Lord? See v. 2

When God's people take the lead, in truth and righteousness, obeying the word of the Lord, to break the chains of oppression and darkness, God is praised.

2. What was the context, before Deborah arose as a mother in Israel? What was the problem?See v. 7 & 8

    Life among the people of God had become drudgery as they succumbed to idol-worship, and did not even fight for their lives, when cruelly oppressed.

3. How was the condition of the heart, of Deborah? See v. 9

    She was in tune with God and was much encouraged to see willing volunteers among the people, who believed the word of the Lord that came through her.

4. What was the role of the singers? See v.10-12

    The singers recited the righteous acts of the Lord, and of His warriors in Israel. They proclaimed victory and alerted the prophetess and the general when the enemy was defeated.

    They were encouragers.

5. How did the tribes of Israel respond to the call to battle? See v. 13-18

    As in Judges 4:6, per the instruction of the Lord, it was the tribe of Naphtali and the tribe of Zebulun who responded to the call to battle, and some came from Ephraim and Benjamin. Issachar also went into the battlefield. The tribes of Reuben, Gilead(half-tribe of Manasseh), Dan and Asher did not take part. We should refrain from speculating on the tribes which were not mentioned: Judah, Simeon, Gad, while the Levites would be carrying out their priestly duties (Numbers 1:49-53).

6. What is being described in v. 19-30?

    The battle in the physical and the spiritual realm was being described-- esp. in v. 20 "From the heavens the stars fought". The worry of Sisera's mother and the vain consolation of her servant girls was also described.

7. Whose victory was it really? See v. 31

It was the Lord's victory, and victory also belonged to those who loved Him, and obeyed His word, bringing peace for forty years in Israel.

8. What is your view/understanding of the prophetic gifting?

This gifting is often affirmation in another person's life, where he/she has already heard from God. It can be directive and specific, or it can be a warning against evil/sinful habits.

It is a gift that God is happy to give those who are loving and responsible. A key verse for the operation of this gift would be Matthew 5:8 "Blessed are the pure in heart, for they will see God." Love and purity would be key characteristics of a God-fearing prophet/prophetess. He/she is also careful to direct praise and glory to God alone, and keep none for self.

9. What are underlying principles that should accompany the gift of prophecy? See 1 Corinthians 14:3, 19-20. See also 1 John 4:1-3

"Follow the way of love" is a key principle in the exercise of this gift, in private/public (corporate worship), all the more in public, as the impact would be great on many personal lives, for good or evil. "Test every spirit" is another principle- is the word of prophecy given in honour of the Lord, acknowledging His Lordship, His life of faith and obedience(come in the flesh, i.e. recognizing Jesus as fully God and fully human)? In 1 Corinthians 14:19-20 the principle/ purpose of giving the word here is the clear edification/instruction of others, and their maturity.

10. How can the church today carry out the exercise of prophecy as instructed by the apostle Paul in 1 Corinthians 14:29-31? What is a key principle here?

The emphasis is on order, respect and edification, and accountability, as two or three prophets (not just just one) should speak, and be willing to let others give more words of revelation. People are to take turns to speak, so that everyone may be edified.

9. Ruth

Part I From despondency to hope

Ruth 1 & 2

This piece of history is set in the period of the judges, where there was famine in Judah, and an Ephrathite from Bethlehem, Elimelech, and his family went to live in Moab. Elimelech died, leaving his wife Naomi and his sons Mahlon and Kilion who married Moabite women. They had lived in Moab for about ten years, and Naomi's two sons died too. She heard of better prospects in Bethlehem, as the Lord provided food for His people there, and decided to go back (Ruth 1:6).

1. At the crossroads, what was Naomi's counsel & prayer for her daughters-in-law? See Ruth 1:8-9

    Naomi tells her daughters-in-law to return to their mothers' home and to seek re-marriage, believing that that would be best for them, praying that God show them kindness.

2. What was their reaction? See v. 9-10

    They both wept and insisted on following Naomi back to her hometown.

3. What was the culture of the day when one's husband has died? And what seems to be the role of the woman in general? See v. 11-13

    Re-marriage would be ideal, and the role of the woman in general was to be a wife and mother.

4. What was the outcome at the crossroads finally? See v. 14-18

    Orpah left Naomi in tears, but Ruth clung on and had made up her mind about following Naomi back to her people.

5. What is evident from Ruth's response to her mother-in-law? See v. 16-17

    She had grown to love her mother-in-law, and come to know her God, Yahweh, and was determined to stay with her.

6. What was the meaning of the name 'Naomi'? What was the condition of her heart upon arriving in her hometown, as she was greeted by her old friends? See v. 20-21

    The meaning of Naomi is pleasantness. Her heart was embittered with the loss of her two sons, and that she returned to her homeland empty.

7. What season was it when Naomi and Ruth returned to Bethlehem? See v. 22

    It was the beginning of the barley harvest.

8. What can you see from Ruth's actions? See Ruth 2:1-3

    She was willing to work with her hands, to support herself and her mother-in-law. She was loving, responsible and humble.

9. What is evident from the exchange between Boaz and his harvesters? See v. 4-7

    Boaz was God-fearing, and people-loving, and his harvesters loved and respected him in return. What a wonderful way to greet one another, in an employer-employee relationship!

Boaz noticed Ruth's presence and found out all about her from his harvesters.

10. Boaz went to speak with Ruth, and showed her kindness. See v. 8-13, how was Ruth's response?

Ruth was grateful that she had found favour with Boaz, and was conscious of her lowly position.

11. What can we learn here about position/ethnic background and its implications, comparing what we see in general in today's society with the way Boaz had treated Ruth? See v. 14-16

In a consumerist and materialistic world people can be rather shallow, and care only for relationship that brings material gains. Ruth was kind to her mother-in-law, and became a daughter-in-substance; and Boaz in turn was kind to Ruth, treating her like one of his own harvesters. Furthermore, racial discrimination/tensions still exist today because it is natural for one to have affinity toward one's own kind. To accept/love/respect people of different ethnic background is almost supernatural. Godly kindness ruled the day for Boaz and Ruth.

12. What did Ruth bring back to her mother-in-law? See v. 17-18

She brought back barley that she had gathered and also food for Naomi.

13. What was Naomi's reaction upon finding out that Ruth went to work in the fields that belonged to Boaz? See v. 20-22

Naomi was thrilled and said a blessing for Boaz, and praised God for showing kindness to them, as Boaz was a close relative, a kinsman-redeemer.

Part II Marriage and genealogy

Ruth 3 & 4

1. What was the intention behind Naomi's instructions to Ruth? See Ruth 3:1-4

   Naomi hoped to secure a good future for Ruth, to find her a new home. She must have known that Boaz was trustworthy and capable, and would be happy to provide for Ruth, and take her as his wife.

2. What was Ruth's response? See v. 5-6

   She agreed and went and did as she had been instructed.

3. What was a key statement in the words of Ruth to Boaz? See v. 8-9

   She was very clear about her identity and his, she was happy to serve, and he was the kinsman-redeemer.

4. What was Boaz's response? See v. 10-13

   He saw it as a kindness, and complimented her noble character. He promised to do his part, and if the closer kinsman-redeemer would pass on the redemption of the estate according to custom, he would do it.

5. What was the significance of the gift of barley for Ruth to take home? See v. 15

   It was assurance for Ruth and Naomi, that he would do his best to settle matters.

6. What can we observe from Naomi's advice? See v. 18

    She was confident that Boaz would do his best, and settle matters that day, when Ruth had returned home. It must have been an assurance from God's presence, as Naomi knew the Lord her God.

7. Boaz went to the town gate and got ten elders together, and invited the other kinsman-redeemer to settle the estate of Elimelech. What can we see from his attitude and his actions? See Ruth 4:1-5

    He respected the customs of the day, and organised a gathering of elders at the town gate, with the other kinsman-redeemer, in order to settle things, for Naomi and Ruth. He trusted God for the best outcome.

8. What was the outcome? See v. 6-10

    The other kinsman chose not to redeem the estate, and gave his sandal to Boaz as a sign authorising him to do it.

9. What was the blessing from the elders and all those present? See v.11

    They said a blessing for Ruth to become like Rachel and Leah, to be fruitful in the womb. It was a blessing of multiplication.

10. Boaz married Ruth and she conceived, and gave birth to a son. How did the women praise God? See v. 15

    They were joyous at Naomi's good fortune, as she had become a grandmother-in-substance. They proclaimed renown for Boaz and the baby, it was in essence bringing glory to God in Israel. They also credited Ruth for being faithful, and a blessing to Naomi. The little boy was a blessing from God, replacing the sons that she had lost.

11. In the genealogy, Boaz was the ancestor of king David. His grandmother was Rahab (the ex-prostitute), and his wife a Moabite who chose to worship Yahweh. What can we see here of God's heart, toward the naming of 'His people'? See Matthew 1:1-6, Genesis 12:1-3

While the Jews are God's chosen people, He has not excluded Gentiles from partaking in the blessing of being His people, and He looks at the heart of a person – He rewards those who are faithful to Him, whether Jew or Gentile. The heart of God towards all nations had been to bless, through Abraham. Our Lord Jesus, a seed of Abraham, was the Word that became flesh, and is present with us today, in His Holy Spirit.

10. Esther

Part I The fall of a queen and the making of another

Esther 1 & 2

1. What was the context described in Esther 1:1-8?

    It was a time when Xerxes(Ahasuerus) reigned over 127 provinces from India to Cush(the upper Nile region), and he had organised an exhibition(conference) over 180 days in the citadel of Susa, his capital city, displaying his wealth and splendour. Thereafter he threw a party for seven days for all the people of the city in his enclosed garden.

2. What was Queen Vashti engaged in and how did she respond to the king's wishes? See v. 9-12

    She too had a party of her own, and declined to oblige when the king sent for her, to show off her beauty to his guests. The king might have drunk too much wine.

3. What were the consequences, and what do you think was the likely reason that led to the consequences? See v. 13-20

    The king was furious and consulted his wisest men, seven nobles from Persia and Media on what to do with Vashti. He was embarrassed in the presence of his guests and 'lost face'.

4. What is a good lesson here for women, especially those who are married?

It is good to consider the feelings and reputation of one's husband, more so in public.

5. What was the edict that was proclaimed after the removal of the queen? See v. 22

Every man should be ruler of his own household, implying that every woman should be careful not to follow the conduct of the deposed queen.

6. How was the king feeling and what advice did he receive from his attendants? See Esther 2:1-4

He felt lonely and started to miss Vashti. They proposed to bring beautiful girls from every province into the harem, to be given beauty treatments, and that the king should select the new queen from amongst them. He was pleased with the advice and agreed.

7. Who was Mordecai and Esther(Hadassah)? See Esther 2:5-7

Mordecai was a Jew from the tribe of Benjamin, and Esther was his cousin, whom he brought up like his own daughter as her parents had passed away. They had been taken into exile when Judah fell into the hands of Nebuchadnezzar, king of Babylon.

8. What happened to Esther, what was her attitude, and the resulting outcome? See Esther 2:8-9

She was taken into the palace with other lovely girls and her attitude was pleasing to the eunuch in-charge, Hegai. He provided beauty treatments, and seven maids from the palace for Esther and moved her to the best room in the harem.

9. How was her relationship with Mordecai? See Esther 2:10-11

    It was a very trusting and close relationship, just like father and daughter, as Esther obeyed Mordecai's instructions and kept her nationality a secret. And Mordecai walked to and fro outside the harem everyday to stay in touch with Esther.

10. What were the customs in the palace for women who were chosen to vie for the position of the queen? See Esther 2:12-14

    Each girl had to complete 12 months of treatments, 6 months with oil of myrrh and 6 with perfumes and cosmetics. She would then go and spend an evening, till morning with the king, with a gift of her choice. She would only return to the king when summoned by name.

11. How was the relationship between Esther and Hegai and the other attendants in the palace? What do you think is the key factor? See v. 15

    She found favour in the eyes of Hegai and all the other attendants, as she was gracious and respected authority.

12. How did the king take to Esther? See v. 16-17

    He was attracted to her more than all the other virgins, and chose her to be queen.

13. How was the coronation celebrated? See v. 18

    The king had a banquet in the honour of the new queen, for his nobles and officials, proclaimed a holiday throughout the provinces and gave out generous gifts.

14. Why was it imperative for Esther's nationality to be kept secret? See v. 20

    The Jews were in exile in a foreign land, and danger was all around, probably because they had their own way of life, e.g. they worshipped Yahweh.

15. What did Mordecai uncover when sitting at the king's gate, and what did he do? See v. 21-22

He overheard a plot to kill Xerxes, and reported the conspirators to Queen Esther, who reported it to the king, giving credit to Mordecai.

16. What was the outcome? See v. 23

The report was investigated and found to be true, and the conspirators were put to death on the gallows. The event was recorded in the annals of the king.

Part II The plight of the Jews

Esther 3, 4 & 5

1. For some reason, Haman the Agagite was honoured by the king, and people were commanded to kneel down and pay honour to him, as the king had made him second in rank, higher than all the other nobles in the land. Why do you think Mordecai refused to follow the instructions? See Esther 3:1-4

Mordecai was a Jew and would not bow/kneel to any other human being, as it was commanded in the ten commandments to worship God only. See Exodus 20:5.

2. How did Haman react? See v. 5-6

He was livid with anger, that Mordecai would dare to oppose his wishes. He schemed to destroy not only Mordecai but all of the Jews. Haman was a descendant of Agag, who lost in battle to king Saul (See 1 Samuel 15:7-9). He was likely overtaken by a vengeful and hateful spirit.

3. What did Haman propose to the king, and on what pretext was it proposed? See v. 8-9

Haman proposed that the king issue a decree to destroy the Jews throughout the provinces, on the pretext that they had their own way of life and that they were disobedient to the king. They were accused of being a threat to the king's best interest. He tried to fund the proposal with his own money.

4. How did the king respond? See v. 10-11

Xerxes believed the words of Haman, gave his signet ring to Haman to issue a decree to carry out the proposal to destroy the Jews.

5. What was the edict proclaimed over the Jews? See v. 12-13

In the language of each people group across the provinces, it was written, that on the 13th day of the twelfth month, the month of Adar, all the Jews, young and old, women and children included, were to be killed.

6. As the king and Haman sat down to drink, what happened in the city of Susa? See v. 15

The city of Susa was bewildered! In other words great trauma came upon them- Jews and non-Jews presumably.

7. How did Mordecai and his people react? See Esther 4:1-3

Mordecai tore his robes, put on sackcloth and ashes and went into the city wailing. The Jews across the provinces mourned, wailed and wept, and many put on sackcloth and ashes.

8. How did Esther react when she heard that Mordecai was wailing in sackcloth? See v. 4-5

    She was distressed by it, and sent clothes for Mordecai to put on instead of sackcloth. She sent her attendant eunuch to go and find out the reason for the mourning.

9. What was Mordecai's urgent request to Esther? See v. 8

    He wanted Esther to go to the king, to beg for mercy and to plead with him for her people.

10. Esther sent word of her situation to Mordecai, which had seemed hopeless as she had not been in the king's presence for 30 days; what was Mordecai's challenge to her? See v. 13-14

    He was overcome with grief, and was stern and warned her not to think only of herself, as God could raise anyone to deliver the Jews from their plight. It was almost prophetic of Mordecai to say that if she were to keep quiet, she would be left out of the deliverance, and her family too will be destroyed. He pointed out that God could have put her in her position as queen just for this very purpose- to speak for the welfare of her people.

11. Did Esther take up the challenge? See v. 15-17

    Yes she did, and instructed a universal fast for her and with her as she prepares to go and see the king in three days.

12. What was the implication here, as Esther instructed Mordecai and all the Jews in Susa to fast with her and her maids for three days?

    They were pleading with the Almighty for favour from the king.

13. What did Esther do on the third day? See Esther 5:1

She courageously went and stood before the king in the inner court, in front of the king's hall though not summoned.

14. What was the king's response? See v. 2-3

He was pleased to see Esther, and held out his sceptre to her, inviting her into his presence, knowing that she came with a request, he offered to grant her up to half his kingdom.

15. Esther did not bat an eyelid at the offer of power over half of Xerxes' kingdom. What can you observe here of her character? See v. 4

She was not interested in selfish gain and knew clearly her purpose, while her people fasted, she focused on saving their lives.

16. Esther invited the king to bring Haman to a banquet, and promised to make her request known. How was Haman's attitude? See v. 11-12

He was thrilled to be invited to Esther's banquet, and boasted to his friends and his wife, of how he had been honoured by the king, his vast wealth, his many sons, and how he was elevated above everyone else in the kingdom. He was foolishly arrogant. And his friends were like him.

17. What was gnawing at his mind, and what advice did his wife and his friends give him? See v. 13-14

Mordecai sitting at the king's gate was an eyesore for him, and his wife and his friends advised him to build a gallows and to ask the king to have Mordecai hanged.

Part III The honour of a hero and the hanging of a villain

Esther 6 & 7

1. King Xerxes could not sleep and read the book of the chronicles. What was he reminded of? See Esther 6:1-3

   He was reminded of Mordecai's kindness/service to him, when he exposed a plot to kill him.

2. What did the king proceed to do? See v. 4-10

   The king decided that honour was due to Mordecai, and proceeded to command whoever in the court at that time to suggest the method of honour and to carry it out. Haman happened to be that very person.

3. Who do you think was behind the whole orchestration of events here? See v. 11-14

   Our Almighty God, without the shadow of a doubt, had been orchestrating these events as the timing of the king's sleeplessness, his reading of the annals and the timing of Haman entering the outer court. See Proverbs 21:1 "The king's heart is in the hand of the Lord; he directs it like a watercourse wherever he pleases."

4. At Esther's banquet, the king again offered to do for Esther whatever she asked; what did she ask for? See Esther 7:1-4

   Again, Esther had no interest in half of the kingdom(power & wealth), but she asked for her life, and the lives of her people, as they have been sold for annihilation.

5. How did the king respond? See v. 5-7

   The king was indignant, and asked who was the culprit who dared to scheme to destroy the queen and her people. Esther exposed

Haman, and finally the king woke up to his own foolishness, and walked out into the gardens in a rage.

6. What did he see when returning from the palace garden? See v. 8

   Haman was begging for his life, and falling on the couch where Esther was reclining; this made the king mad and added another reason for him to execute Haman, i.e. for dishonouring the king and queen.

7. Harbona one of the attending eunuchs voluntarily announced a possible punishment for Haman; does it surprise you as he seems to have been waiting for the chance to tell of what Haman had done? See v. 9-10

   Not at all, as Haman had probably made life miserable for the people around him, e.g. those who served in the king's palace, with his scheming and boasting; and there are those who would speak up and stand up for righteousness at the opportune time.

8. What had been a weakness of the king which made him vulnerable to the manipulation of those with evil intent?

   He was keen to show off, and probably had loved to listen to lies that puffed up his ego. And so he became an instrument in the hands of evildoers.

Part IV Deliverance and celebration

Esther 8, 9 &10

1. What did Esther continue to do, and how was her heart towards her people? See Esther 8:1-6

   Esther was given the estate of Haman, and she told the king of how she was related to Mordecai, and made Mordecai in charge of the estate. She continued to plead humbly with the king for the welfare of the Jews.

2. What was the king's instructions? See v. 8-10

    The king commanded a new decree to be written, overruling the previous one, with Mordecai's orders to the Jews and all the officials of the 127 provinces.

3. What was granted to the Jews in the new edict, on the same day on which they had been sold for destruction? See v. 11-12

    They were granted the right to assemble and protect themselves, to destroy, kill and annihilate any party that might attack them, their women and children, and to plunder their enemies.

4. How did Mordecai leave the palace having accomplished his duties, and how did the people in the city respond to the new edict? See v. 15-16

    He was clothed in royal garments of white and blue, with a crown of gold on his head, and also robed in fine purple linen. The city of Susa celebrated the new decree, as the Jews had been spared, and honoured.

5. How had the tables turned for the Jews when the thirteenth day of the month of Adar came? What was Mordecai's role? See Esther 9:1-4

    The Jews attacked those who sought their destruction and with the backing of the king's edict, their enemies were subdued easily. Mordecai was feared among the people and he became more powerful.

6. Why do you think the Jews chose not to take the plunder? See v. 10, 15, 16

    This author believes that it was for remaining faithful to Yahweh, that they chose not to take the plunder even when they were given the right to do so; as the livestock and the goods of their enemies may have been dedicated in pagan worship.

7. The king again offered to do whatever Esther requested; what was her request? See v. 13-15

    Esther requested that the edict be effective for one more day in the city of Susa, so that the ten sons of Haman can be captured and hanged. The king agreed and it was done.

8. What is the significance of Purim, and how was it celebrated? See v. 18-22

    It was a day of rest, and feasting with joy, commemorating the day of deliverance from annihilation. They celebrate by giving food to one another, and also giving gifts to the poor. It was celebrated annually on the fourteenth and fifteenth days of the month of Adar.

9. What was the final end for Xerxes and Mordecai? See Esther 10:1-3

    The kingdom of Xerxes flourished and grew in power and might, as he could impose tribute throughout the provinces; and Mordecai must have been of great assistance, being second in rank. It was a good ending for Xerxes, Mordecai and the kingdom that was recorded in the annals of the kings of Media and Persia.

11. Summary and conclusion

These Bible studies have been written with the aim of applying age-old principles in today's world, where human beings struggle with sin, Christians wrestling often without the knowledge of the Word of God, or a commitment to walk in godliness and power ("For the kingdom of God is not a matter of talk but of power" 1 Corinthians 4:20 (NIV)). I have been receiving Scripture through numbers repeating themselves, through daily living (e.g. a friend's mobile phone being switched on at 10:27 when sitting next to her on the train, and 10:27 seeming to jump out at me from the clock on my personal computer at work, and Isaiah 10:27, John 10:27, Luke 10:27, Mark 10:27 and Matthew 10:27, coming alive when I read these verses on different occasions in a span of six months); with the leading of the Holy Spirit, the sense of witness within my spirit in agreement, with awe and excitement but also with much peace. I believe God is calling His people to return to the Word as it is imperative to be properly equipped spiritually, mentally and emotionally, living in such interesting times. We need to spend devotional times in God's presence, and we also need to study His Word, and be strengthened, to be effective vessels for Him wherever we are placed.

Why study these five women in the Old Testament? A woman of God at church used to call me Rebekah or Rachel interchangeably, and others have done it too, while my name is really Deborah (a name which God gave for my baptism at the age of 21). I asked the Lord, 'am I to be like Rebekah/Rachel?' And Ruth is a character I admire as she stuck with her mother-in-law, and chose to follow the ways of Yahweh, when she had no obligation to do so. Esther has always been special, and more so since the birth of the Association of Christian Accountants, as I was led by the Holy Spirit to study the book and prepare for the visit with the delegation of Christian accountants to Beijing – the forerunner event which led to the birth of the ministry. And it certainly is good to study Deborah the judge, prophetess and peacemaker from whom the inspiration was drawn for my own new name at baptism. At that time I just wanted to be hardworking, like a bee, as that's what 'Deborah' means in Hebrew (*smile*).

I have noticed a general phenomena among women – the whining, complaining, comparing, criticizing and gossiping; which I have not been keen on, knowing that it is not good for spiritual growth and fellowship in the body of Christ. I have also attended Christian conferences for women, where there seems to be a common set of problems that define women (the speakers liked to begin their messages with this as introduction), and I have often felt out of place. And I determined to be like Jesus, and to go back to the Bible for truth. God in His grace, per original design has made man and woman good, with his and her particular roles to fulfill (see Genesis 1: 22-24). When Adam and Eve fell, distortion of these roles have come in as well, and the curse of God came upon the land and man and woman. Yet God did not give up, and continued to instruct His people, walking with them, providing for them, protecting them from their enemies, and bringing them into the promised land, Canaan. The role of women was important too, in the Old Testament while customs seemed to have put them in second place, making the man more important. And so confusion about equality between man and woman, has its roots in customs that are carried out blindly, without understanding from the heart. The Almighty has been speaking to me repeatedly about the heart, in the past 2-3 years, that **He wants our hearts to be strong and tender. And He wants the church to be strong and pure, not lame and weak, overladen with many sins.**

When we look at the lives of the five women, we cannot ignore the people around them, and so we need to study personalities like Isaac and Jacob and Laban for example. I hope to bring a holistic perspective into the lives of these men and women, and I pray that women will truly know **who we are in Christ** and live victoriously for Him, as Jesus has won the victory. We are covered by His righteousness, and His righteousness is being worked out in us daily as we choose to walk in faith and obedience. According to Romans 8:17, **we are heirs together with Christ**, "And if children, then heirs; heirs of God, and joint-heirs with Christ; if so be that we suffer with him, that we may be also glorified together" (KJV). And thank God for Proverbs 31! When I read it, my soul is strengthened and I am grateful for the godly standard put forth by this passage which had been a queen mother's advice to her son, the king. The five women studied in this little project had not been perfect, and they were all living under the grace of God.

Rebekah started out really well, and her betrothal story is heartwarming. Then came the twin babies, and conflict had already begun in her womb. Both Isaac and Rebekah stumbled in their parenting as they each favoured one twin over the other. We see the hand of God and the grace of God at work in their lives as he allowed scandal, and heartbreak; to bring them to the place of peace and reconciliation. And God's word to Rebekah stood the test of time as Jacob was ultimately blessed to be the succeeding patriarch figure after Isaac.

Rachel competed with her sister in her own strength, giving her maid as a concubine to Jacob, and Leah followed suit, thus Jacob ended up with twelve sons. It is worthwhile to note that God could have granted Jacob, Rachel and Leah twelve sons without their interference! She displayed more immaturity when she stole her father's idols, lied and invited a curse from her own husband. Yet, God was gracious and when the time was ripe, He opened her womb and gave her two sons, Joseph and Benjamin. Years later, she was remembered in the book of Jeremiah as the mother of Israel's children (descendants), a prophetic symbol for intercessors, travailing in prayer for the people of God. God's discipline is evident in the lives of Jacob & Rachel, and so is His grace and mercy. Jacob became Israel, cleansed his house of idolatry, and started afresh.

Rachel was buried in Bethlelem, and God sent His Son Jesus to be born of a virgin in Bethlehem.

Deborah was a judge (peacemaker), a prophetess, a leader and a wife. She was one who heard clearly from God, and spoke His word of instruction to Barak, God's appointed general who would lead the armies of Israel to defeat their oppressor. Her life was marked by war and peace. We can learn from her to be bold and courageous, when we are called to be His mouthpiece. And to trust God for victory and peace. Spiritual warfare is real, but our victory has been secured; we need to trust and obey, when the Holy Spirit says: conquer! God's special word to the men through this historical record, is this: honour will follow when you trust and obey Him.

Ruth the Moabitess came from a people group who did not worship Yahweh, and having married a son of Naomi, a Jewess, she chose to leave her old ways, to follow her mother-in-law, and her ways, after the death of her husband. She chose to worship Yahweh, and stuck with her mother-in-law who had become very dear to her, committing herself to work, and to provide for her. Her kindness was rewarded as she happened to meet Boaz, a well-respected and wealthy kinsman-redeemer. We see the grace and kindness of our Almighty God at work, as customs were dealt with respectfully and the desire of the heart was granted for Boaz and Ruth. They became the ancestors of king David, and our Lord Jesus, born hundreds of years later.

Esther the orphaned child who grew up under the care of her cousin Mordecai, was taken to the palace of the king, during dangerous times, as the Jews had been taken into exile. She found favour in the eyes of Hegai the eunuch in charge of all the virgins undergoing beauty treatments, preparing themselves to see the king. Esther also found favour with all the other attendants in the palace. The king took a certain liking to Esther and made her queen. While Yahweh was not mentioned in the book, His hand at work cannot be denied, as the chain of events which brought about truth, justice and mercy for His people could not be pure coincidences. Mordecai and Esther depended on the Almighty and became agents of deliverance, turning a day of calamity into a day of celebration, and Purim continues to be celebrated among the Jews to commemorate the great deliverance. Therefore, today we have hope even when darkness surrounds, as we persevere in faith and obedience, He will bring truth, justice and mercy.

A special note

Jeremiah 31 speaks of God's new covenant with Israel and Judah, where He promises justice and mercy. There is redemption, repentance, return, rebuilding and rest for the remnant. The knowledge of Him will be for every man and woman, from the least to the greatest. Past sins are forgiven and forgotten. His people will return to their homeland and rebuild their lives. Literally this applies to Israel as a nation, and spiritually this applies to the New Testament church. We see a culmination and fulfillment as many more Jews return to Israel to re-settle, and many more Jews receiving Jesus as Lord and Saviour. Our Lord Jesus came in the flesh, and fulfilled this word of prophecy that came through Jeremiah, and opened the way for Jews and Gentiles to be reconciled to God (see also Isaiah 2:1-5). God kept His covenant when He sent Jesus. "The Word became flesh and made his dwelling among us. We have seen his glory, the glory of the One and Only, who came from the Father, full of grace and truth." (John 1:14)(NIV) When Jesus walked on earth, He demonstrated grace and truth, through His relationships, His teaching and His healing of the sick and demon-possessed. He became our example for life on earth. And so, in this life we should be like Him, and live in the light of the second coming (see 1 Thessalonians 4:13-18), every Christian awake and ready, to receive his/her Lord when He comes. Come Lord Jesus!